Reginald Heber, Frederic B. Schell

**From Greenland's Icy Mountains**

Vol. 1

Reginald Heber, Frederic B. Schell

**From Greenland's Icy Mountains**
*Vol. 1*

ISBN/EAN: 9783337289638

Printed in Europe, USA, Canada, Australia, Japan

Cover: Foto ©Andreas Hilbeck / pixelio.de

More available books at **www.hansebooks.com**

"FROM GREENLAND'S ICY MOUNTAINS"

# FROM

# GREENLAND'S ICY MOUNTAINS.

BY

REGINALD HEBER.

———

20 ILLUSTRATIONS BY

FREDERIC B. SCHELL.

———

PORTER & COATES,

PHILADELPHIA.

# List of Illustrations.

DRAWN BY FREDERIC B. SCHELL.

ENGRAVED UNDER THE SUPERVISION OF JAMES W. LAUDERBACH.

# ILLUSTRATIONS.

FROM GREENLAND'S ICY MOUNTAINS.

F ROM
Greenland's
icy mountains,

F<small>ROM</small>

India's

coral strand,

WHERE Afric's sunny fountains
Roll down their golden sand,

From many an ancient river,

FROM many a palmy plain,
They call us to deliver
Their land from Error's chain.

WHAT though the spicy breezes
   Blow soft o'er Ceylon's isle,

THOUGH every prospect pleases,
And only man is vile?

IN vain with lavish kind-
ness

The gifts of God are
strown:

THE heathen, in his blindness,
  Bows down to wood and stone.

CAN we, whose souls are lighted
  With wisdom from on high—

CAN we to men be-
nighted

The lamp

of life

deny?

SALVATION! O Salvation!
   The joyful sound proclaim,

TILL each remotest nation
    Has learnt Messiah's Name.

W AFT, waft, ye
winds, His story,
And you, ye waters, roll,

TILL like a sea of glory
  It spreads from pole to pole—

TILL o'er our ransom'd
nature
The Lamb for sinners slain,

REDEEMER, King, Creator,
In bliss returns to reign.